YOU choose

Don't Be Sad, Sam

It's OK

Lisa Regan

It might be useful for parents or teachers to read our 'How to use this book' guide on pages 28-29 before looking at Sam's dilemmas. The points for discussion on these pages are helpful to share with your child once you have read the book together.

First published in 2013 by Wayland

Copyright © Wayland 2013

Wayland
338 Euston Road
London NW1 3BH

Wayland Australia
Level 17/207 Kent Street
Sydney, NSW 2000

Produced for Wayland by Calcium
Design: Emma DeBanks
Editor for Wayland: Victoria Brooker
Illustrations by Lucy Neale

British Library Cataloguing in Publication Data

Don't be sad, Sam. — (You choose)
  1. Sadness—Juvenile literature.
  I. Series
  152.4—dc23

ISBN: 978 0 7502 7707 5

Printed in China

Wayland is a division of Hachette Children's Books,
an Hachette UK company.
www.hachette.co.uk

Contents

Hello, Sam!

Like other children, Sam sometimes gets **sad**. He doesn't want to be **unhappy**. But now and then sad things happen that make Sam want to **cry**.

Follow Sam as he finds himself
in situations in which he feels **sad**.

YOU choose too!

Be brave, Sam

Oh, no! Sam drops a plate while helping Dad with the washing up.

The plate smashes into
pieces on the ground.
Dad looks really **upset**
and a little bit **cross**.

What should Sam choose to do?

Should Sam:

- shut himself in his bedroom?

b say sorry to Dad and help to pick up the pieces (then have a cuddle)?

c curl into a ball and cry?

Sam, choose **b**

Grown-ups **understand** that **accidents** happen. If they are upset, it is because of the accident, not because of you. If they seem cross, try to remember that they are not cross at you.

What would **you** choose to do?

9

You can cry, Sam

Sam's pet **hamster** has **died**.

He knows that hamsters
don't live as long as people,
but he still feels like **crying**.

What should
Sam choose
to do?

Should Sam:

a stay awake all night **sobbing**?

b sit on his own and **refuse** to play with anyone?

c have a little cry and a big cuddle with Mum?

Sam, choose **c**

It's normal to feel sad when someone or something dies. Crying lets other people know that you are sad – then they can help you. After you've had a good cry, dry your tears and remember the good times.

What would YOU choose to do?

Stay friends, Sam

Sam's best friend Jonas is moving to a different town.

Sam doesn't want
Jonas to go away.

What should
Sam choose
to do?

Should Sam:

a plan to talk to Jonas on the computer after he moves?

b stop talking to his friend?

c say he has a tummy ache and can't go to school so he doesn't have to see Jonas?

Sam, choose **a**

It's okay to feel upset when someone goes away. You have to try harder to stay friends with people you don't see every day. Play with your other friends to help cheer you up, and make sure you keep in touch with the people who have moved away.

What would you **choose** to do?

Join in, Sam

Sam is watching his **classmates** in the playground.

He feels **left out** of their game.

What should Sam choose to do?

Should Sam:

a sit behind a tree away from all of the children?

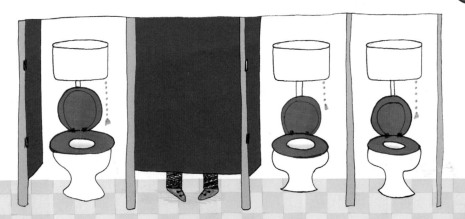

b lock himself in the toilet and feel sad?

C ask if he can join in with the others?

Sam, choose **C**

No one wants to feel left out. But usually people aren't trying to leave you out, they're just getting on with their game. Be **brave** and let them know that you want to join in.

What would you choose to do?

Speak up, Sam

Sam thinks his parents **love** his sister more than him.

It seems like they always
do things with her.

What should
Sam choose
to do?

Should Sam:

a pack his bags to run away from home?

b ask his Dad if they can do something fun together?

c stop talking
to his Mum
and Dad?

Sam, choose **b**

Don't ever feel sad
by yourself. **Explain**
how you feel to the
person who is making
you sad. Once they
know what is wrong,
they can try to help.

What would
YOU
choose
to do?

Well done, Sam!

Hey, look at Sam! Now he can knows what to do, he's feeling much **happier**.

Did you choose the right thing to do? If you did, big cheers for you!

If you chose some of the other answers, try to think about Sam's choices so you can stop yourself from feeling too sad next time. Then it will be big smiles before long!

And remember – it's okay to feel sad for a while because things will get better soon.

How to use this book

This book can be used by a grown-up and a child together. It is based on common situations that can affect any child. Invite your child to talk about each of the choices. Ask questions such as 'Why do you think Sam should talk to someone when he feels sad?'.

Discuss the wrong choices, as well as the right ones, with your child. Describe what is happening in the following pictures and talk about what the wrong and right choices might be.

● Don't be scared to tell someone you're sad. They can't help you to feel better if they don't know how you feel.

● Running away doesn't ever help. You may still feel sad inside, even if you are far away from whatever is making you sad.

● Crying helps bad feelings to come out and helps you to feel better.

● Try not to feel sad for too long. Crying for a very long time can just make you feel worse.

Ask your child to tell you what makes them feel sad. Discuss things that make you feel upset, and tell them how you feel inside. Explain that it's okay to have these feelings, and that it happens to just about everyone.

Encourage your child to talk about their feelings rather than keeping them secret. Ask them if crying helps, and if they feel like they need a cuddle. Help your child to learn what makes them feel better, and which people they trust to talk to about how they are feeling. Let your child know that it's fine to feel sad sometimes, but that it is important to have fun times, too!

Glossary

accidents things that happen
  without you meaning them to, such
  as breaking a plate or falling over

brave to feel strong enough to
  do something that seems scary

classmates children in your class

explain to show how something works

hamster a small, furry animal that
  is kept as a pet

refuse to not do something when asked

sobbing to cry so hard that it hurts

understand to know something

unhappy to feel sad

upset to feel sad

Index

Titles in the series

ISBN: 978 0 7502 7706 8

Like all children, Annie sometimes gets really, really angry! She has lots of choices to make – but which are the CALM ones?

ISBN: 978 0 7502 6724 3

Like all children, Carlos sometimes does things that are wrong, and doesn't come clean. He has lots of choices to make – but which are the TRUTHFUL ones?

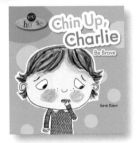

ISBN: 978 0 7502 6722 9

Like all children, Charlie sometimes feels a little scared. He has lots of choices to make – but which are the BRAVE ones?

ISBN: 978 0 7502 6725 0

Like all children, Gertie sometimes plays a little dirty. We put Gertie on the spot with some tricky problems and ask her to decide what is FAIR!

ISBN: 978 0 7502 6723 6

Like all children, Harry sometimes takes things that don't belong to him. He has lots of choices to make – but which are the HONEST ones?

ISBN: 978 0 7502 7709 9

Like all children, Henry sometimes gets angry and sometimes he hits, too. He has lots of choices to make – but which are the GENTLE ones?

ISBN: 978 0 7502 7707 5

Like all children, Sam sometimes feels sad, and he doesn't know how to make himself feel better. He has lots of choices to make – but which are the HAPPY ones?

ISBN: 978 0 7502 7708 2

Like all children, Tilly wants to do everything *right now*, and sometimes she just can't wait! She has lots of choices to make – but which are the PATIENT ones?